The Dao of Teaching

The Dao of Teaching

Designing Lessons to Harness the Learning
Power of Nature

Wilma J. Maki

Canadian Cataloguing in Publication Data

The dao of teaching: designing lessons to harness the learning power of nature
by Wilma J. Maki

ISBN 978-0-9733426-3-5
eBook ISBN 978-0-9733426-4-2

Published by Wilma J. Maki
White Rock, BC, Canada

Cover design by manish414
Front cover photograph by Wilma Maki
Back cover verse: From Roger T. Ames and David L. Hall,
Daodejing: Making This Life Significant
Verse next page: From Burton Watson, *The Complete Works of Zhuangzi*

First Edition: August 2022

'The inborn nature is the substance of life. . . .'
Zhuangzi, chapter 23

Contents

Introductory Notes

1. This book uses the pinyin (PY) system for the Romanization of Chinese script. The pinyin system has become the standard system in recent decades devised as a phonetic system based on Mandarin. Another system widely used is the Wade-Giles (WG) system. Conversions to the Wade-Giles system are noted when the words are introduced, e.g., Daoism (Taoism WG).

2. The word dao is not capitalized in the book. This reflects the interpretation of dao as it appears in the everyday of our lives and does not discount the natural transcendent character of dao that also inspires spiritual and physiological interpretations. The word is not italicized as it is now in common use in most Western societies.

3. References to verses and excerpts in the book are as follows with further details in the endnotes:

   Verses from the *Daodejing* (*Tao Te Ching* WG) are taken from Roger T. Ames and David L. Hall, *Daodejing: Making This Life Significant.* The authors use the word 'way-making' to express the meaning of dao.

   Excerpts from *Zhuangzi* (*Chuang Tzu* WG) are taken from Sam Hamill and J. P. Seaton, *The Essential Chuang Tzu,* and Burton Watson, *The Complete Works of Zhuangzi.*

CHAPTER 1

Daoist Education in Context

Way-making gives them life and nurtures them,
Rears and develops them.
It brings them to fruition and maturation,
Nourishes and guards over them.

Daodejing, chapter 51[1]

The Promise of Nature

'Way-making [dao] gives them life and nurtures them,' is the promise of nature expressed in the notion of dao in the text, *Daodejing*. Bringing this promise to children in our education is the goal of this book.

The desire to bring nature into one's life rests on an understanding of nature, not as the other of humans, but as a process that when functioning correctly is the most specialized and powerful system for human wellbeing. This understanding underlies a recent movement in our society of looking to nature to define physical and spiritual wellness, activities of daily living, and treatment of disease. Accessing nature's specialized and powerful system is also the reason for bringing it to teaching and learning.

The philosophy of Daoism is a popular source for understanding and using the power of nature. However, it is most often understood through the lens of a Western worldview and placed in a mystical framework that is an integral part of the view. Understanding the character of Daoist ideas within its own world takes time, and recent re-evaluations of the standard texts have moved in that direction.

What we now understand is that as the Daoist ancients applied their view to various human purposes, they did not ignore one of the most important human functions—how we know and create our realities. We can now read the *Daodejing* from an educational perspective to define dao learning and teaching practices to cultivate it.

The Dao of Teaching is an introduction to Daoism as an educational treatise for the purpose of designing lessons for student learning with nature.

Entering a classroom with a dao lesson taking place will look like a regular class in session, however, on closer examination we find that the learning is different.

The learning is an interchange between student and lesson in alignment with nature, and while different, it can be considered the functional equivalent of traditional learning methods. As learning is a process, it can be applied in any subject and level according to the discretion of the teacher, as well as in learning situations outside of the classroom. Teaching dao lessons is easy to learn and does not require expertise in the Daoist philosophy or one of its practices.

Learning aligned with nature is a natural way to see, understand, and live in one's world. It is learning at one's highest potential. This is a desired outcome, but there are other very important benefits.

When learning with dao, nature defines the relationship between student and lesson environment, fostering the development of deference for the environment and an understanding of the interdependence between the two, thereby creating a worldview for sustainability. And perhaps most important is that invested in the process is the confirmation of a deep fondness for the child and sacredness of life in the pursuit of authenticity of both the person and the earth.

What the Book is About

The Dao of Teaching is set up in a simple format outlining the core concepts of the Daoist philosophy that are essential for teaching lessons and then providing practical lesson examples to assist teachers in applying them. It defines dao learning and the teaching practices to cultivate it, and explains how this information is used to design a basic 3-step lesson and five variation lessons. The book serves as a guide for teachers to design lessons for student learning with nature.

The main ideas that frame the book are as follows:

- Dao is defined as nature's design for humans in search of definition. It is nature's specialized way for humans to see, understand, and live in their world.
- The main reference, *Daodejing*, provides definitions of dao learning and teaching practices to cultivate it.
- When comparing the Daoist ideas with John Dewey's definition of experience, we find many similarities, an association first noted by Dewey himself.
- These findings are used to bring dao learning to the teaching of lessons.
- Dao lessons can easily be applied to regular lessons. They are designed to work with and complement current teaching practices, not to replace them.

As we learn about the Daoist approach, we find that it is not as foreign as one might initially imagine. Many aspects of dao teaching and learning are similar to ideas we now hold. Also familiar to most is the Daoist method of using specific forms to align a human purpose with nature, as in the practices of tai chi or acupuncture. Importantly, the Daoist approach is to be used at the teachers' discretion, occasionally or frequently, as tai chi is to callisthenics or as acupuncture is to our traditional medicine.

And, as we learn about the Daoist approach, we begin to understand that teaching with dao does not mean we must move to the forest. The forest is a teacher of nature, but we can also bring the forest to the classroom. This does not mean bringing the trees or plants to the classroom, it means bringing the character of the forest to the classroom—the forest as nature, as in all parts in genuineness, in interdependence and processual, and using these characteristics to structure the lesson activity.

The Philosophy of Daoism and the West

Daoism is a worldview based on nature, but a definition of nature that is different from how Westerners most commonly see it as the other of humans. Daoists define nature as the ongoing and provisional process of all matter, a process they named 'dao.' Humans are part of this process, not separate, not higher or lower, but open to seeing, contributing, and receiving in co-creation with their environment.

Because of different levels of familiarity with Daoism, this section gives a brief overview of the origins of the philosophy, and its adoption in the West and in education studies.

Daoism is an indigenous philosophy of China believed to have originated in the teachings of the legendary Yellow Emperor of China (ca. 2700 BCE) and Laozi (Lao Tzu WG, the old master). In the second century BCE, it became one of the 'Hundred Schools of Thought' in China's golden age of intellectual development.

The two main texts are the *Daodejing* and *Zhuangzi*. The *Daodejing* is often attributed to Laozi, but many believe that it was written by numerous Daoist scholars over a period of time. *Zhuangzi* is named after the author, ca. 360–280 BCE.

Daoism is one of the two most important philosophies of China, the other being Confucianism (Confucius, 551–479 BCE). The two philosophies have influenced lifestyle and thought in China and its neighbouring East Asian countries to present day.

Daoism was first introduced to the West in the 1500s. The *Daodejing* was given to the Jesuits and a translation was kept in Rome with only a few people access to it. It is interesting to note that of these few, some of the most renowned in the history of

Western thought, such as Georg W. F. Hegel and Carl G. Jung, were well informed on the subject of Daoism.

Today, Daoist texts are readily available. Asianist Theodore de Bary, for example, states that the *Daodejing* has been translated into more foreign languages than any other Chinese work.[2]

Educators are also looking to Daoism as a resource for new ideas. It is mainly used as a reference for contemplative and holistic studies, and for an approach to give voice to our natural environment. However, the philosophy has rarely been considered for the practice of teaching lessons.

What We Have Learned

It was only a few decades ago that many Westerners saw Daoist practices as a kind of witchcraft or new-age gibberish, but such views have been replaced with a more comprehensive understanding of the philosophy. Some of the findings stand out as they pertain to education and are discussed next as they form the basis of the book.

Daoism as a Resource in Education

Daoism is one of many possible sources of a worldview of nature from different times and geography, but it offers several advantages.

The Daoist view is relevant to human affairs with its focus on the relationship between humans and their environment. The school also includes descriptions of how to apply nature to different human purposes, covering areas from spirituality to war, to such daily functions of what to eat and what to wear. It has a long history of study and practice, and most critically, the findings are documented in a canon of almost 1500 texts. The availability of these texts today make Daoism an excellent resource for studies of nature.

As the Daoists applied their view of nature to different human purposes, there is no doubt that they also applied their ideas to education, and these are found in the *Daodejing*. Sinologists Roger T. Ames and David L. Hall explore the text from an educational perspective in *Daodejing: Making this Life Significant*, and it is an understanding of this interpretation that is the primary reference for this project.

Ames and Hall suggest that the main purpose of the text is to give instructions on how to create a disposition for dao in the becoming process in humans. The becoming process is the natural and ongoing transformations of experiences that regulate how we know and create our realities.[3]

The characterization of the process defines learning, and the instructions define the teaching practices. This provides the information for bringing nature to the teaching of lessons.

Dao as Nature's Learning

The idea that dao describes nature's specialized way of learning is made clear in the opening chapter of the *Daodejing*. Dao is 'how one observes the mysteries of all things.' Looking at Daoism from this perspective, it might even be suggested that education is at the very heart of the philosophy.

Educators have often looked to nature as a resource for ideas. In the 1700s Jean-Jacques Rousseau taught his student Emile with nature as the guide, and Dewey followed with his definition of experience.

It is not surprising then that dao learning can be understood as similar to Dewey's experience. As noted, it was Dewey himself who saw a link between his characterization of experience and dao, stating in *Experience and Nature*, 'Such facts have been celebrated by thinkers like Heracleitus and Lao-tzu.'[4] Scholars studying Daoism also find similarities between dao and experience, expressed by Joseph Grange as, 'Experience is the living tissue of the *dao*.'[5]

Because of the similarities found between the Daoist and Dewey's views, frequent comparisons are made to help situate the Daoist characteristics in education. Like Dewey's experience, dao learning is child-centered, focuses on inquiry and self-directed learning, and adapted to the development stage and needs of the child.

Also like experience, learning takes place between the learner and lesson environment, with the environment regulating the learning. In both, the energy for learning lies in the process, not in an external agent.

We can also now understand dao learning from a scientific perspective. Fritjof Capra in his book, *The Tao of Physics*, describes the movement of atoms of individual matter and energy of the universe in quantum mechanics as a process of creation that resembles dao.

Daoist Teaching Practices

The instructions to the sage in the *Daodejing* on how to create a disposition for dao define the teaching practices.

The practices are familiar to most as they include the main concepts of the philosophy, such as the practices of 'letting go' and creating emptiness. While these practices are different from those we usually associate with teaching, we now understand their characteristics as they relate to learning.

Understanding the characteristics of the teaching practices is important, however equally important is understanding when, where, and in what combinations to apply them. This information can be gleaned from the *Daodejing*.

We find that the teaching practices are not used alone, rather, they work as a system, each depending on the others to become Daoist in character.

We also find that the practices are not directed at the learner, but at the environment part of a learning activity to create an environment aligned with nature.

It is the nature environment in the lesson activity that becomes the agent to regulate the learning, while the teacher is the catalyst.

Dao Lessons

What we have learned about dao learning and Daoist teaching practices, as well as their similarities and differences with experience, allows us to bring dao learning to lessons as Dewey brought experience to lessons.

And, predictably, the main structure of the lessons is similar. Both look to the students' environment to regulate the learning, and both give the teacher the job of designing this environment. Though similar in basic structure, each had different ideas about the role of the teacher. Dewey's teacher is to design the lesson for growth, whereas the Daoist teacher is to design the lesson aligned with nature.

While the *Daodejing* gives the characteristics of teaching and learning with dao, ideas for the lesson designs in the book come from a variety of sources. Some come from personal experiences in teaching and research, and some are from others' work. These sources provide the designs for a basic 3-step lesson plan and five variation lessons.[6]

The one criterion in all of the designs is that dao learning defines the learning in the lesson activity. However, an important characteristic of a dao lesson is that the dao learning can dovetail with other kinds of learning, not only in other lessons, but also within the dao lesson itself. Choosing one over another is not part of the Daoist view, and this inclusiveness leaves open possibilities for the teacher's own creations.

Dao Lessons in Context

The dao lessons are not presented as a replacement of current teaching practices.

Transmission of knowledge from our ancients is part of educating the young. It is the memory that is passed from one generation to the next, however, we must also understand that nature exceeds this memory which has its boundaries drawn by its genealogy. Teachers have a curriculum to teach, but they also have an option to teach lessons using the process of nature learning.

Zhuangzi's story of student Yan Hui (Yen Hui WG) is an example of how dao learning can be situated in a traditional education setting.

The Story of Yan Hui

Hui is a student of Confucius, and under such tutelage studied the classics of ancient wisdom. Hui tells Confucius that he has decided to go to the court of the Prince of Wei. He explains that he feels it is his duty to help the suffering of the people under the rule of the irresponsible prince, and says how he will deal with the prince.

> Although my words may instruct or reprimand, they are the words of the ancients, not my own. If I manage things just so, although I am upright, I will not be blamed.

This is what I mean by being a companion of the ancients. If I can be just so, will that work?

'It will *not*,' Confucius replied.

Confucius thought Hui was not ready although he was his student and had learned a great deal. Without dao he could lose his virtue in search of fame, or if he tried to keep his virtue, relying on the words of the ancients, he would surely get hurt, might even lose an ear or die. Until Hui could know the way of dao, he would not be ready for the prince's world.

Sometime later Hui returns to meet Confucius. Confucius now believes he is ready to go.

Now I can say to you, you may enter and go rambling around in that cage of his and yet remain untouched by fame and honours. . . . In the service of men, it's easy to be false, in the service of nature, it's difficult. …

If you keep eye and ear connected to what's inside, and keep heart and mind and knowledge outside, the very spirits of earth and air will throng to dwell within you, and how much more will mere men then be drawn to you? This is the ten thousand things, everchanging.[7]

The Book Outline

The book is set up as a practical guide for teachers for putting dao lessons into practice.

As a first step, the next chapter gives three exercises that have been set up to clarify one's views on educating. This will allow for comparisons with those in the Daoist approach to help identify what practices and ideas need to be shifted to teach dao lessons. The chapter closes with a discussion and a sidelight.

Chapters 3 and 4 present descriptions of dao learning and teaching practices as the background knowledge needed for designing dao lessons. Understanding the characteristics of dao learning is also necessary for teachers to be able to judge if it is actually taking place in the learning activity. Understanding the characteristics of the teaching practices and how they work is also necessary to ensure the right conditions for dao learning. The chapters close with a discussion, summary of the main points, and a sidelight.

With this background knowledge, chapter 5 outlines a basic 3-step dao lesson plan. Chapters 6 and 7 give variations of the lesson. Each lesson plan begins with the lesson objective, followed by descriptions of the three steps. Next, an example lesson is given to show how the dao lesson can be applied to a regular lesson. The chapters close with a discussion, summary of the main points, and a sidelight.

Chapter 8 discusses teaching dao lessons in context.

Sidelight: The Innate Spirit

The marsh pheasant will go ten steps for a single peck of food and a hundred for a single sip of water, but you can't beg him into eating once he's caged. Though he may be a king in spirit, it does no good.

Zhuangzi, chapter 3[8]

CHAPTER 2

Identifying Values
and Perceptions of Education

In carrying about your more spiritual and more physical aspects
   and embracing their oneness,
Are you able to keep them from separating? . . .

In scrubbing and cleansing your profound mirror,
Are you able to rid it of all imperfections?

Daodejing, chapter 10[9]

A Starting Point

'In scrubbing and cleansing your profound mirror,' teachers continuously evaluate their practices. What are the effects of one's teaching, not only for academic performance, but also for fostering personal wellbeing?

A useful starting point in the study of the Daoist approach to teaching is to clearly define the values and perceptions one holds about education. This chapter provides three exercises that are set up to explore these views.

The first exercise is to plan a simple lesson. The next charts the values one assigns educational goals, and the third, one's perceptions about how we learn.

Beginning with a clear view of how and why one plans lessons in a particular way allows for comparisons with the dao lesson. The example lesson in the exercise is the same one that will be used when introducing the dao lesson in chapter 5. This will help identify any differences to determine what teaching practices to keep and what ones need to be altered. It will also show how a regular lesson can easily be adjusted to create a dao lesson.

The exercises also give insight to connections between how one plans lessons and the values and perceptions one holds about education. Comparing them with those in the Daoist approach will help identify what views one needs to shift to design the dao lessons.

Exercise 1: Lesson Planning

The first exercise is to design a lesson for a simple mathematics question.

Lesson: 2-digit by 1-digit multiplication for grade three students

Each box contains twelve candies.
There are five boxes of candies. How many candies are there?

Situation

Students have learned:

Addition and subtraction up to four digit numbers
Multiplication with single digit numbers
Multiplication with base ten

The above basic mathematical skills have been taught using any teaching method. The methods might include column forms, base ten blocks, worksheets, and videos.

Lesson Plan

Step 1: Set-up

_____

_____

_____

Step 2: Lesson Activity

_____

_____

_____

Step 3: Closing

_____

_____

_____

Exercise 2: Educational Goals

This exercise is set up to identify the values one assigns educational goals. It lists nine educational goals.[10]

Comparing one's values with the educational goals associated with the Daoist approach in the following chapters will help reveal any shift in views needed to teach dao lessons.

Identifying the goals one values most highly can also help one understand associations between the choices and how one designs lessons. After finishing the exercise, one can consider associations between one's assigned goals and the lesson plan in the previous exercise.

Identifying Values of Educational Goals

From the following list of educational goals, which do you consider the most important, second most important, and third most important.

Building basic literacy skills (reading, writing, math)
Encouraging academic excellence
Promoting vocational skills
Promoting good work habits and self-discipline
Promoting personal growth and fulfillment
Promoting human relations skills (team work)
Promoting specific moral values
Promoting ability to solve problems on one's own
Promoting education for sustainability

The three most important goals are:

1. _____

2. _____

3. _____

Exercise 3: How People Learn

This exercise is set up to clarify the perceptions one holds about how people learn. It lists four main methods of learning and one 'other' category.

Charting the relative value one gives each learning method will help identify the similarities and differences with the character of the learning in dao lessons.

After finishing the exercise, one can return to the previous exercises to consider associations between the ideas one holds about how people learn, educational goals, and lesson plans.

Identifying Perceptions of How People Learn

Indicate your perception of how people learn with a percentage so that the total is 100 percent.

The methods of learning are: 1. Experience (learning from doing a task); 2. From teachers (courses, lectures); 3. From peers (collaboration with others); 4. On own (individual experiments, research); 5. Other.

1. Experience   _____ %

2. From teachers   _____ %

3. From peers   _____ %

4. On own   _____ %

5. Other   _____ %

Total   100 %

Discussion

Teachers will hold different values and perceptions about education.

Some teachers might already be teaching lessons that resemble the Daoist approach, and some teachers' lessons will be quite different. Some teachers will have few changes to make when designing a dao lesson, while others more, and some might not want to let go of the views they now hold.

There is no right or wrong in one's choices.

The exercises are set up to help one better understand the character of the dao lesson. Dao lessons offer students another way of learning and are not meant as a replacement or disruption of current educational progress. As will be explained in the next chapters, dao learning works with other learning methods.

Sidelight: The Teacher

I went to the woods because I wished to live deliberately, to front only the essential facts of life, and see if I could not learn what it had to teach, and not, when I came to die, discover that I had not lived.

Walden [11]

CHAPTER 3

Dao as a Learning Process

There was some process that formed spontaneously
Emerging before the heavens and the earth. . . .

All pervading, it does not pause. . . .

If I were to style it,
I would call it way-making (*dao*).

Daodejing, chapter 25[12]

Dao and Learning

'There was some process that formed spontaneously,' it is called dao and extends to all matter. In keeping with this definition, dao includes the natural process in humans in search of definition.

This chapter will explore what dao is, its character in learning, and the learning in the context of a lesson. To teach lessons with dao, one must first understand what dao is to judge if it is actually occurring in the lesson. Understanding its characteristics also determines what teaching practices and lesson designs are needed to cultivate it.

Most people are already familiar with many of its characteristics. Scholars liken it to Dewey's definition of experience, quantum mechanics, and the human imagination. These provide references for understanding dao as a learning process.

The Word Dao

We can begin to understand dao by thinking of it simply as the word chosen by the ancient Daoists to convey what they observed in nature.

We can also begin to understand what the ancients observed by looking at the writing character they chose for dao.

道

The character is made up of two elements with origins in pictorial lettering.

The element on the left side is a foot. We can picture the foot as moving forward. This element by itself is translated as 'to pass over,' 'to go over,' and 'to lead through.' The element on the right is a head, showing hair and eyes (originally drawn horizontally). This element also has a meaning of going forward, and is translated as 'foremost' and 'to lead.' Dao is the continuous forward movement of the foot and head on a pathway often referred to as 'the way.'[13]

The images of the foot and head in the word dao are consistent with how the ancients described it. The *Daodejing*, chapter 25 (chapter introductory verse) defines its main characteristics.

Dao is a verb, not a noun. It is a process, and as such, a 'way,' but not a set path to follow. The process is ongoing and encompasses all matter.

Dao is the process of creation in nature. Humans, as part of nature, are transient as is all matter.

Scholars express the character of dao in various ways.

Ellen M. Chen defines it as movement, 'the everlasting rhythm of life, the unity of the polarity of non-being and being.'[14] Ames and Hall describe it as dao-ing or 'way-making,' the processual and provisional becoming process of experience.[15]

Defining the Dao Process

Dao is the word used to describe nature's ongoing process of creation of non-being to being. But what exactly is the character of this process that will also define learning with dao?

Zhuangzi describes the process in his story of Cook Ding (Ting WG). Ding is a butcher and displays his craft for Lord Wen-hui.

> Ting the cook was cutting meat free from the bones of an ox for Lord Wen-hui. His hands danced as his shoulders turned with the step of his foot and bending of his knee. With a shush and a hush, the blade sang following his lead, never missing a note. Ting and his blade moved as though dancing to "The Mulberry Grove," or as if conducting the "Ching-shou" [Jingshou PY] with a full orchestra.
>
> Lord Wen-hui exclaimed, "What a joy! It's good, is it not, that such a simple craft can be so elevated?"

Ding explains that it is not skill that guides his knife. Rather, he meets the ox with his whole spirit, finding the way of dao that is beyond skill. His knife is led by the natural makeup of the hollows and openings of the ox, never touching the ligaments or bones. His work with dao is like a dance, moving effortlessly, harmoniously, and with the highest degree of efficiency. Ding adds that it took years of practice to perfect.[16]

Scholars describe the process in various ways. Capra explains it in terms of quantum mechanics. He recalls his first experience with the molecules and energy of the universe in what he calls a 'gigantic cosmic dance.' 'I "saw" the atoms of the elements and those of my body participating in this cosmic dance of energy; I felt its rhythm and I "heard" its sound.' The metaphor of the dance, he notes, is sometimes used in modern physics and some Eastern views to express the process of creation and nature.[17]

Ames and Hall describe the process as a co-creative process of shaping and being shaped. They use a soup imagery to portray it.[18] There are many ingredients in a soup, and each interacts with other ingredients to change and produce new flavours and scents.

The examples characterize the creation process. It is Ding's work with dao, the cosmic dance, and shaping and being shaped. They describe the act of non-being to being and a phenomenon that draws our attention.

However, considering Ding's example, we see that the process includes three parts—a past, an interaction, and an outcome. The past is Ding's past experiences that he brings to the work, the interaction part is exemplified in the interaction between Ding and the ox, and the outcome is the butchered ox and another experience for Ding.

The three parts make up the whole that characterizes the dao process. It is the application of this whole that helps us define dao in learning and lessons.

Dao in Learning

There is no doubt that the ancient Daoists saw dao as the natural process in humans to gain a perception of a reality of one's unique world. The human mind, as all other matter, experiences the process of dao. As Ames and Hall state, the human imagination is the clearest example of how dao works.[19]

How the dao process would appear in a learning activity can be explored by first looking at Dewey's definition of experience. As mentioned, scholars have found that it is similar in many aspects.

Dewey gives a description of the process in experience in his example of an artist at work in *Art as Experience*. The interaction is between the artist and canvas. There is no person directing the process, nor is there a predetermined outcome directing the project. The artist uses both his mind and emotions as he explores the canvas and decides each stroke. As the paint is applied, the canvas changes, and each time it changes the artist reacts to the new character of the canvas. The artist paints each brush stroke in the moment with acknowledgment of the past. Both the artist and canvas are in a process of shaping and being shaped.

The main ideas in dao learning are similar to the artist at work and follow the character of the three parts of the dao process. The learning takes place between the individual and his/her environment with no outside input or predetermined outcome directing the activity. The learning is part of an ongoing process of shaping and being shaped, as one brush stroke creates a new situation that again needs exploration. The individual brings his/her past to each interaction as does the artist, but the past does not steer the process. The outcome is open to the creation of a myriad of possibilities, as is the painting.

Dewey and the Daoists describe a similar process. The central notion in experience is that it is a transactional process that takes place between the individual and his/her environment. This is the same in the dao process.

In both, it is in this interaction that there is creation. As explained by Ames and Hall, the 'energy of transformation lies within the process itself rather than in some external agency.'[20] Both also describe similar conditions in the interaction. Dewey states that it is one of attunement of the participants in a situation, as in the artist reacting to each change on the canvas.[21] The Daoists describe it as entailing the genuineness, the innate characteristics of the participants in a situation.

The interaction defines the central notion of experience and dao in learning. However, as seen in the examples of Ding's work and the artist, the past and outcome are tied to the interaction. These also need to be defined as they also take part in characterizing dao in learning.

The Daoists make it clear that the past is an integral part of the interaction. This is stated in the *Daodejing*, chapter 2 as the 'before and after lend sequence to each other,' and chapter 14 as:[22]

Hold tightly onto way-making in the present
To manage what is happening right now
And to understand where it began in the distant past.
This is what is called the drawstring of way-making.

It is natural that we bring our ideas to the present moment. The past will be part of dao in learning, however, it takes on a particular character in the process as seen in the examples of Ding and the artist. It is present, and is used, however, it does not steer the interaction. It is suspended so that the individual can explore the moment. In nature, the moment exceeds the past to direct the interaction.

The third part of the dao process, the outcome, has two distinct characteristics that are also parts of dao in learning. One is that it is open to a myriad of possibilities. This is the wonder, joy, and excitement of the process as described in Zhuangzi's story of Hui as 'the ten thousand things, everchanging.' Two, the outcome is not limited to the individual. The outcome immediately creates a new situation to shape it, and again be shaped.

The three parts that make up dao learning are used to structure the lessons.

Dao Learning in Lessons

Dao learning is brought to lessons as Dewey brought experience to lessons. Knowing the character of dao learning, we can begin to see how it will define the basic structure of lessons.

The three parts of the dao learning process will affect the lesson design as follows:

- The past is brought to the learning activity, but how it is acquired does not define its character. This means that the past is open to any teaching method.
- The interaction part defines the lesson activity. The activity is between the learner and lesson environment in their full genuineness.
- The outcome creates a new situation, and this situation can be used to continue the learning. It is also open to any teaching method.

The learning that occurs in the activity dovetails with other learning methods before and after the activity. This adheres to one of the core concepts in Daoism that opposites actually work together, as stated in the *Daodejing*, chapter 2, 'This is really how it all works.'

> High and low complete each other,
> Refined notes and raw sounds harmonize (*he*) with each other,
> And before and after lend sequence to each other—
> This is really how it all works.[23]

Thus, a distinguishing feature of dao learning in lessons is that it dovetails with other learning methods according to the definitions of the past and outcome that are specific to the dao process. It is the definitions and inclusion of these two parts in the process that begin to differentiate dao learning from Dewey's experience.

Dewey and the Daoists both looked to the teacher to cultivate the learning, but each had their own ideas for the role of the teacher. This would also play a part in creating differences between the two approaches.

The Daoist teaching practices, as given in the *Daodejing*, are introduced in the next chapter.

Discussion

Dao defines the natural process in humans in search of definition. The learning takes place in the interaction between humans and their environment in a process similar to Dewey's experience. Its three parts of a past, interaction, and outcome are used to inform the basic structure of lessons.

In the lessons, the learning dovetails with other methods before and after the activity. Including a mixture of learning methods in one's view differentiates it from progressive views, including Dewey's, that focus on replacing top-down methods with bottom-up learning. This characteristic explains how the dao lesson works with current teaching practices.

It is important to remember that humans take an active role in the dao process. Our image of 'letting go' in Daoism is often interpreted as simply allowing a situation to go in an undetermined direction. However, the definition of dao makes it clear that humans participate with body and mind with the participants of the environment, each shaping and being shaped. Humans are an integral part of the process as illustrated in the examples of the artist and Ding.

An understanding of the dao process reveals a worldview for sustainability that is implicated in the character of the relationship between humans and their environment. The relationship is defined by nature to ensure the genuineness of each of the participants, and harmony with and deference for one's environment.

Chapter Summary

The main characteristics of dao learning are as follows:

- Dao learning is nature's design for humans in search of definition.
- It can be understood as the workings of the imagination, similar to Dewey's experience, or as quantum mechanics.
- The learning takes place between the individual and his/her environment.
- It entails the genuineness of the participants in the interaction.
- The learning is within the interaction process, not from external sources.
- The past is part of the process, but does not steer it.
- The outcome is also part of the process. It is open to a myriad of possibilities and creates a new situation.
- The past, interaction, and outcome inform the basic structure of the lesson.
- The dao learning in the lesson dovetails with other learning methods.

Sidelight: An Intimate Relationship

During his reign, Huang Di [Huang-ti WG, the Yellow Emperor] discoursed on medicine, health, lifestyle, nutrition, and Taoist cosmology with his ministers Qi Bo, Lei Gong [Lei Kung WG], and others.

Huang Di said, "From ancient times it has been recognized that there is an intimate relationship between the activity and life of human beings and their natural environment. The root of all life is yin and yang; this includes everything in the universe, with heaven above and earth below, within the four directions and the nine continents."

"The three months of the spring season bring about the revitalization of all things in nature. It is the time of birth. This is when heaven and earth are reborn. During this season it is advisable to retire early. Arise early also and go walking in order to absorb the fresh, invigorating energy. . . . On the physical level it is good to exercise more frequently and wear loose-fitting clothing. This is the time to do stretching exercises to loosen up the tendons and muscles. Emotionally, it is good to develop equanimity. This is because spring is the season of the liver, and indulgence in anger, frustration, depression, sadness, or any excess emotion can injure the liver. Furthermore, violating the natural order of spring will cause cold disease, illness inflicted by atmospheric cold, during summer."

The Yellow Emperor's Classic of Medicine [24]

CHAPTER 4

The Teaching Practices

Hence in the words of the sages:

We do things noncoercively (*wuwei*)
And the common people develop along their own lines;
We cherish equilibrium (*jing*)
And the common people order themselves;
We are non-interfering in our governance (*wushi*)
And the common people prosper themselves;
We are objectless in our desires (*wuyu*)
And the common people are of themselves like unworked wood.

Daodejing, chapter 57[25]

Instructions to the Sages

'Hence in the words of the sages,' this is how to teach. Leave the people as unworked wood. The unworked wood is a metaphor in Daoism depicting the innate qualities of an entity and the natural power in that state.

The opening lines of chapter 2 in the *Daodejing* describe the problem in society and premise for the text. People had moved away from the way of nature and divided the world.

> As soon as everyone in the world knows that the beautiful are beautiful,
> There is already ugliness.
> As soon as everyone knows the able,
> There is ineptness.[26]

You sage, it states, are to follow these instructions to fix it. The authors of the text make it clear that sages are not to simply escape from society to the mountain top. They had a critical role to play in society as teacher.

There is no doubt that the authors thought the role of the sage as teacher was very important. It is defined right after the introduction to the philosophy in the first chapter, and before instructions are given for self-cultivating practices, the most common interpretation of the text.

It was because people had moved away from nature that the Daoists believed they needed instructions to return to nature. As they designed postures in qigong to bring the body to a natural state for wellbeing, they designed teaching practices to bring the people to a natural state for learning.

This chapter defines three teaching practices that the *Daodejing* gives for creating a natural state for learning. Most people are already familiar with them as they are the core concepts of the philosophy of non-action and emptiness.

The chapter describes the practices as they relate to learning, and also states where, when, and how they are applied. The Daoists applied the practices in a very specific way and this is key to using the practices in lessons. This information is also given in the *Daodejing*.

The Daoist teaching practices are also explored in comparisons with Dewey's ideas. As would be expected, the general approach is similar, however, the roles for the teacher would differ.

The Three Teaching Practices

The *Daodejing* describes three teaching practices to cultivate a natural state for learning. Knowing the character of dao learning from the last chapter, that the past and outcome parts of the process are open, we can understand that the practices will be directed at the interaction part of the process.

The three practices are non-action (*wuwei*), no-knowledge (*wuzhi, wu-chih* WG), and no-desire (*wuyu*). While there are many more *wu* practices in the Daoist view, these three can be used to structure the lessons to ensure the conditions for dao learning.

The *wu* part in the words means 'in an absence of,' characterizing the practices. The absence does not indicate non-existence, but rather a lack of being present. The written character, below, has the meaning of absence. The bottom element is the radical for fire giving the character its general meaning. The top element is phonetic, also found in the character of the word *wu* 舞 meaning dance.

無

The first teaching practice is given to the sage in chapter 2 and is one of the most important concepts in Daoism—the practice of non-action (see also this chapter introductory verse).

> It is for this reason that sages keep to service that does not entail coercion (*wuwei*)
> And disseminate teachings that go beyond what can be said.[27]

The instruction for teaching is defined. The practice of non-action, commonly known as 'letting go,' means that the teacher is not to interfere in the interaction between the student and his/her environment. The second sentence further characterizes this practice. Non-action is teaching without words.

Chapter 3 defines two more teaching practices—the no-knowledge and no-desire practices.

> Ever teaching the common people to be unprincipled in their knowing (*wuzhi*)
> And objectless in their desires (*wuyu*),
> They keep the hawkers of knowledge at bay.
> It is simply in doing things non-coercively (*wuwei*)
> That everything is governed properly.[28]

The instructions for teaching are defined. The practice of no-knowledge means that another's knowledge should be absent in the interaction. The practice of no-desire means that any unnatural desire should also be absent in the interaction.

The three absence practices produce a natural state for learning. Any input of the teacher, another's knowledge, or unnatural desire would give one part of the interaction more power than another, diminish the authenticity and capacity of the participants, and sway the process in an unnatural direction.

The practices allow the interaction to be solely between the individual and his/her environment according to the definition of the dao process. Each participant in the interaction contributes in its full genuineness to harness the natural power of unworked wood.

Refining the Images of the Absences

Protecting the innate is at the heart of teaching with dao, establishing and preserving the natural relationship between humans and their environment. As Zhuangzi explains:

> The inborn nature is the substance of life.
> The inborn nature in motion is called action.
> Action that has become artificial is called loss.

Zhuangzi, chapter 23[29]

The *wu* absences are often misinterpreted when viewed from a Western perspective. Educators, in particular, are understandably wary of embracing a practice named no-knowledge, or teaching with non-action to students with no desire.

However, the *Daodejing* provides descriptions of the practices so that we can understand their function as agents for learning. The descriptions are given in this section, and instructions on how to apply them are given in the next section.

The Non-action Absence

The sage's non-action does not advocate no action, rather, the opposite. The practice is to create action, but a specific kind of action that Zhuangzi states is not artificial and a loss.

The non-action absence as a teaching practice is to not interfere in a student's interaction in the lesson activity. At first, it might be difficult for teachers to imagine that their input is not the critical agent for student learning, however, the Daoist non-action is a productive action precisely for that purpose.

In chapter 2 of the *Daodejing*, after the authors instruct the sage to practice non-action, they explain how it works.

> The sages develop things but do not initiate them,
> They act on behalf of things but do not lay any claim to them,
> They see things through to fruition but do not take credit for them.
> It is only because they do not take credit for them that things do not take their leave.[30]

The sage is to practice non-action to ensure that 'things do not take their leave' so that they can contribute in their full genuineness in the interaction.

Zhuangzi's story of Lord Spontaneity describes the character and importance of non-action. There were three rulers, the ruler of the North Sea, South Sea, and Center known as 'Spontaneity.' The North and South rulers noticed that Spontaneity did not have the seven holes in his body for seeing, hearing, eating, and breathing. They, with all kind intentions, said, 'Our friend here has none of these. Let us try to bore some holes for him.' Each day they bore one hole. On the seventh day, Spontaneity died.[31] For the Daoist, any input for steering, however well-meaning, however seemingly scientific, is the boring of holes in Spontaneity.

The No-knowledge Absence

The Daoist no-knowledge absence does not advocate ignorance. It is simply directed at certain kinds of knowledge. The kinds of knowledge that are to be eliminated are those that are constructed by humans as products of discrimination, such as theories, laws, principles, and rules.

The no-knowledge teaching practice is to ensure that these kinds of knowledge do not steer the interaction in the lesson activity.

The Daoists believe that knowledge that comes from others creates one's reality according to the other person's reality. It is learning on the right side of convention. The result is a veneer of technical wisdom and morality. They explain that adopting others' ideas happens when one's connection with nature is lost. It is both impoverishing and dehumanizing, as expressed in the *Daodejing*, chapter 38.

> As for ritual propriety, it is the thinnest veneer of doing one's
>   best and making good on one's word,
> And it is the first sign of trouble.
> "Foreknowledge" is tinsel decorating the way,
> And is the first sign of ignorance.[32]

The teacher is to 'keep the hawkers of knowledge at bay' so that each participant in the interaction of the activity is contributing in its full genuineness. It is keeping those people away who profess to have the answers and truths.

Zhuangzi's story of Nanrong Zhu (Nan-Jung Chu WG) describes the world of adopted ideas. Zhu was studying Daoism, but his teacher's words would not go past his ears. His teacher could do no more, exclaiming 'I've said all I can say. The saying goes, mud daubers have no power to transform caterpillars. … Now I'm afraid my talents are not sufficient to bring about any transformation in you. Why don't you go south and visit Laozi?' In desperation, Zhu journeyed seven days and seven nights to Laozi's place.

Upon arrival Laozi asked him, 'Why did you come with all this crowd of people?' Zhu looked around, but saw no people. He carried with him the many ideas of others.

'You are confused and crestfallen,' Laozi said, 'as though you had lost your father and mother and were setting off with a pole to fish for them in the sea. You are a lost man—hesitant and unsure, you want to return to your true form and inborn nature, but you have no way to go about it.'[33]

While the no-knowledge teaching practice is to keep the hawkers of knowledge away, the Daoists acknowledge that individuals bring their ideas to the dao process. As noted in the description of dao learning, these ideas are not omitted, rather they are suspended as the individual explores the present moment.

The No-desire Absence

The Daoist no-desire absence does not advocate apathy. It, like the no-knowledge absence, is directed at certain kinds of desires.

The no-desire teaching practice is to ensure that these kinds of desires do not steer the interaction in the lesson activity.

The desires that are to be eliminated are desires to possess or control, such as desires for material goods, fame, or wanting to rule the world, as these desires disregard the genuineness of the participants and direct the activity in an unnatural direction. Living one's life directed by unnatural desires happens when one has lost the way of nature, and like the no-knowledge absence, it is impoverishing and dehumanizing.

The Daoist stand against greed is very strong, as stated in the *Daodejing*, chapter 46.

> There is no crime more onerous than greed,
> No misfortune more devastating than avarice.
> And no calamity that bring with it more grief than insatiability.[34]

Their stand against controlling others is expressed in chapter 29.

> If someone wants to rule the world, and goes about trying to do
>   so,
> I foresee that they simply will not succeed.
> The world is a sacred vessel,
> And is not something that can be ruled.[35]

While the no-desire teaching practice is to remove unnatural desires, the need for desire is acknowledged in the first chapter of the *Daodejing*. This desire is the desire of the artist at work, and the means to define the boundaries of a situation.

The three teaching practices of non-action, no-knowledge, and no-desire set the conditions for dao learning in lessons and Zhuangzi's action.

Applying the Teaching Practices

Creating the right conditions for dao learning is not done by simply 'letting go.' The Daoists gave specific instructions to the sage on how to apply the absences. These are explained next as they are used to structure the lesson.

Instructions for Applying the Absences

The *Daodejing* gives two application procedures.

1. The teaching practices are components of a system.
2. The practices are directed at the environment part of the interaction.

1. *The Practices are Components of a System*

The three absence practices are components of a system, parts of a whole, as presented together in the *Daodejing* chapter 3 and several other verses in the text. Each practice depends on the others to be characterized as Daoist. Using only one will not support dao learning, as one position in qigong, such as adjusting one's feet, will not produce alignment of one's body with nature.

If the non-action teaching practice is used alone, it is not necessarily a Daoist practice. In the Daoist approach, the teacher uses non-action when the no-knowledge and no-desire absences are in place. This determines the timing. This is when the teacher 'lets go' and gives the moment wholly to the student and nature, without mediation.

Some progressive education approaches use teacher non-action to promote learning that is directed by students' personal interests. While this attends to the child, from a Daoist point of view, this would put the activity in a world regulated by conventions of knowledge and desires, such as fixed ideas about beauty, wealth, heroes, and theories that could lead the learning in an unnatural direction. Dewey also believed that teachers simply 'letting go' would not support experience.[36]

2. *The Practices are Directed at the Environment*

The Daoists directed the three practices at the environment part of the interaction, not at the individual. The environment would act as the agent for generating dao learning.

Looking to the environment to generate learning is not a new idea in education. Both Rousseau and Dewey used specific environments for this purpose. The Daoist use of the environment embodies Rousseau's focus on eliminating societal input and also Dewey's focus on designing a particular environment to regulate the learning. The Daoists would eliminate societal inputs with the absences to create a natural environment, and use this environment to generate dao learning.

This defines the Daoist role for teachers. The teacher is to plan a lesson activity that is characterized by the three absences. To create the condition of no-knowledge, the *Daodejing* says to 'keep the hawkers of knowledge at bay.' To eliminate unnatural desires, it gives the following suggestions in chapter 3.

> Not promoting those of superior character . . .
> Not prizing property that is hard to come by . . .
> Not making a show of what might be desired.[37]

The teacher's work is done before the activity and behind the scenes. The non-action is practiced in the activity of the lesson only when the two other absences are in place.

In dao lessons, the teacher is the catalyst, while nature is the agent for the learning.

How the Application Procedures Work

The teacher creates the natural state in the lesson environment of the activity. This, in turn, creates a mirroring effect to produce a natural state in the students.

The natural environment and its mirroring effect ensure the genuineness of all participants in the activity interaction. Ames and Hall summarize this process as follows: 'The mirroring activity that we associate with the Daoist *wu*-forms is a kind of active and nurturing understanding that allows things to shine forth as themselves, both in their transitoriness and in their particularity, without mediation.'[38]

We are familiar with the mirroring effect when viewing a beautiful sunset, bathing in a forest, or entering a cathedral or temple. We are aware of a change taking place in us. Tan Twan Eng, author of *The Garden of the Evening Mist*, describes this change when entering a Japanese garden. 'The same can be said of any work of art, any piece of literature or music. . . . your emotions are *not* being manipulated—they're being awakened to something higher, something timeless. Every step you take inside Yugiri [garden name] is meant to open your mind, to lead you to the heart of a contemplative state.'[39]

From this perspective, we can think of the Daoist teaching approach as another practice in contemplative studies.

The Teaching Practices in Lessons

Dao learning sets the basic structure of the lessons, and the teaching practices further structure them as follows:

- The three absence teaching practices are used to create a natural state for dao learning. They are directed at the environment part of the interaction between the student and his/her environment. The teacher plans a lesson activity ensuring the absences.
- All three practices are applied as they work as a system. The teacher practices the non-action absence only when the no-knowledge and no-desire absences are in place.

This provides the information that is needed to structure a dao lesson. A basic lesson design is given in the next chapter.

Discussion

The *Daodejing* defines three teaching practices to create learning that is not based on discrimination, accumulation, or wanting control the world.

We can understand the Daoist approach to educating as an 'absence approach.' This approach is different from the philosophies that we are most familiar with that entail lengthy study of doctrines to gain knowledge.

The absences can make some educators uneasy, but we know that they create a specific kind of action that Zhuangzi describes as one's 'inborn nature in motion.' We also know that the teacher has a job to do, but it is behind the scenes, and the teacher can use other methods before and after the learning activity. The absences do create some vagueness and chaos, which can also make some educators uneasy, but these are kept in check by the requirement of genuineness of all of the participants. The approach is a functional process that has possible learning potential beyond conventional methods that are bound by their genealogy.

In the Daoist and Dewey's approaches, the teacher designs the lesson environment, but how each does this differs. The role for the teacher in the Daoist approach rests on the view that nature is the best environment to create natural learning. In Dewey's approach, the teacher designs the environment to direct growth, and then guides students during the activity.

Dewey presents his ideas for the teacher's role in his writings. Learning, he states in *Experience and Education*, begins with the child, but the adult's knowledge 'represents the goal toward which education should continuously move.'[40] He explains that the teacher 'is quite likely to know more clearly than the child himself what his own instincts are and mean,' and guidance is simply a 'stimulus to bring forth more adequately what the child is already blindly striving to do.'[41] From Dewey's viewpoint, this is not external imposition, but the means to fulfill the child's experiential learning and normal development.[42] But compared to the Daoist teacher, Dewey's teacher's hand is in the soup. It has purpose and would be the death of Lord Spontaneity.

The characterizations of dao learning and teaching practices can be used by teachers to plan lessons on their own. To guide this process, the next three chapters offer some example lessons.

Chapter Summary

The main characteristics of the Daoist teaching practices are as follows:

- There are three teaching practices to enable dao learning—non-action, no-knowledge, and no-desire absences.
- The three absences are components of a system.
- The teacher applies the absences to the lesson environment to align it with nature.
- The natural character of the lesson environment creates a mirroring effect on students ensuring genuineness of all of the participants.
- The genuineness in motion is action.
- The genuineness keeps vagueness and chaos in check.
- Dewey's role for the teacher to direct the learning with purpose differs from the Daoist reliance on nature.

Sidelight: A Wall of Compassion

I really have three prized possessions that I cling to and treasure:

The first of these is compassion,

The second, frugality,

And the third is my reluctance to try to become preeminent in the world.

It is because of my compassion that I can be courageous;

It is because of my frugality that I can be generous;

It is because of my reluctance to try to become preeminent in the world that I am able to become chief among all things. . . .

When nature sets anything up

It is as if it fortifies it with a wall of compassion.

Daodejing, chapter 67[43]

CHAPTER 5

A Basic Dao Lesson

It is only because it requires unprincipled knowing (*wuzhi*)
That they do not understand me.

But if those who understand me are rare,
I am to be highly prized.
Thus the sages dress in burlap
Yet conceal jade in their bosom.

Daodejing, chapter 70[44]

Designing a Dao Lesson

'Thus the sages dress in burlap,' describes the teacher who is teaching with dao. In a dao lesson, the teacher's work is not displayed for all to admire. The teacher is behind the scenes keeping the jade hidden.

This chapter outlines a basic dao lesson. There are three steps in the lesson following a traditional lesson layout. The definitions of dao learning, absence practices, and application procedures inform the character of each step. The chapter describes each step and then gives an example lesson.

The example lesson is the same mathematics question that was used in the exercise on lesson planning in chapter 2. This allows for comparisons and also highlights how a dao lesson can easily be applied with a few changes to lesson plans that teachers are currently using.

While the main structure of the dao lesson resembles current lessons, it differs in several main ways. Most apparent is the learning activity that is defined by absences. The closing step is also different. Current lessons usually use the closing step for review and evaluation, but learning continues in the dao lesson. Also, particular to the dao lesson is the mixing of the dao learning with other methods of learning.

Variations of the basic lesson are possible and are given in the next two chapters.

The Basic 3-Step Lesson Plan

This section describes each step in the lesson.

The basic lesson plan is used when the teacher wants to teach new material and wants students to develop the new ideas on their own.

The main characteristics of the steps are as follows:

Step 1: Set-up

The teacher plans a lesson activity characterized by the three absences.

Step 2: Lesson Activity

Students interact with the lesson environment and the teacher practices non-action.

Step 3: Closing

Students continue learning by sharing their outcomes with other students and the teacher.

Step 1: Set-up

The teacher plans the lesson activity.

- The teacher reviews the new learning situation.
- The teacher reviews the students' knowledge.
- The teacher plans an activity that is defined by the absences.

The teacher begins with the same questions as in current approaches. What is to be learned and what do students know?

While the two approaches begin in the same way, how each use this information differs. In current approaches, the teacher uses this information to plan how to introduce the new material to students. In the Daoist approach, the teacher uses this information to design an activity aligned with nature.

The teacher starts by reviewing the new learning situation and identifying the participants that make up the situation.

Next, the teacher assesses the students' knowledge that will define their past in the lesson. The question the teacher asks is not how the students learned this knowledge, but rather if the students have knowledge of all of the participants in the new learning situation. If the teacher determines that the students do not have the whole of this knowledge, the teacher must first supply it using any teaching method. Leaving out any of the participants of the new situation would be interference from an outside agency, creating an unnatural environment.

When the teacher determines that the students have access to all of the participants, the teacher plans the lesson activity ensuring the absences.

The step follows the definitions of dao learning, teaching practices, and their application procedures.

Step 2: Lesson Activity

Students participate in the lesson activity.

- The teacher introduces the lesson activity.
- Students participate in the activity.
- The teacher practices non-action.

As in current approaches, the teacher might begin the lesson with a review and then introduce the lesson activity. From that point on, students work on their own and the teacher practices non-action.

The class setting will look like most class settings today, but the learning will be different. The students' past knowledge is brought to the activity, but does not steer it. The learning in the lesson is between the students and their natural environment. The outcome is not defined.

The learning is individual, not group learning. Students are left to develop new ideas on their own terms, and if a student does seek help, the teacher will encourage the student to work it out on his/her own.

Compared to current approaches, the teacher will generally spend less time on presenting material, and students will spend more time on their own.

The step follows the definitions of dao learning, the non-action teaching practice as interdependent with a natural environment, and the use of the lesson environment for regulating the learning.

Step 3: Closing

Learning continues in the closing step.

- Students share their outcomes with other students and the teacher.
- The outcomes can also be viewed in other related contexts.

Typically, teachers use the closing step to review, evaluate what students have learned, and to assign homework.

In the dao lesson, each student has created an outcome and new situation. The step uses the new situation to continue the learning.

Students share their outcomes with other students and the teacher in a process of ongoing interactions and learning. In this step, the teacher is an active participant, directing discussions and giving summaries of the different views.

The students' outcomes can also be explored in other contexts, such as in relation to future projects or to similar projects in society. This can help the students understand how the lesson activity is connected to these projects.

It is rare to give homework in a dao lesson.

The step follows the definition of the outcome of dao learning and the character of dao learning dovetailing with other learning methods. The closing step exemplifies the ongoing movement in the dao process.

Example Lesson

The following is the mathematics question from chapter 2.

Lesson: 2-digit by 1-digit multiplication for grade three students

Each box contains twelve candies.
There are five boxes of candies. How many candies are there?

Situation

Students have learned:

Addition and subtraction up to four digit numbers
Multiplication with single digit numbers
Multiplication with base ten

The above basic mathematical skills have been taught using any teaching method. The methods might include column forms, base ten blocks, worksheets, and videos.

Lesson

Step 1: Set-up

The teacher reviews what is to be learned, 2-digit by 1-digit multiplication.
The teacher reviews what the students know.
The teacher determines that the students have the knowledge of all of the participants in the new situation.
The teacher plans an activity with the absences.
The activity is to give students the problem and have them solve the problem on their own.

Step 2: Lesson Activity

The teacher opens with a review.
The teacher presents the new problem.
The students work on their own.
The teacher practices non-action.

Step 3: Closing

The students give five different ways to solve the problem.

$12 + 12 + 12 + 12 + 12 = 60$
$5 \times 9 = 45, 45 + 5 + 5 + 5 = 60$
$4 \times 5 = 20, 4 \times 5 = 20, 4 \times 5 = 20, 20 + 20 + 20 = 60$
$3 \times 5 = 15, 9 \times 5 = 45, 15 + 45 = 60$
$2 \times 5 = 10, 10 \times 5 = 50, 10 + 50 = 60$

The teacher leads a discussion and summarizes the main points.
The teacher gives examples of how the multiplication can be used when shopping.

Discussion

The *Daodejing*'s descriptions of dao learning and teaching practices are used to design a 3-step lesson plan. In the set-up, the teacher ensures all participants in the new learning activity are free from unnatural influences. Students participate in the activity in the second step, and explore their outcomes in the closing step.

The example multiplication lesson allows for comparisons with the lesson plan exercise in chapter 2. The example shows how easy it is to apply the dao lesson to a regular lesson with a few changes.

Comparing current typical lessons with the dao lesson shows that in the first step, instead of the teacher planning how to present the new material, the teacher prepares a lesson activity aligned with nature. In the activity, instead of the teacher leading the activity, students participate in the activity on their own. In the closing step, instead of the teacher evaluating what has been learned, students share their outcomes. Importantly, the dao lesson combines the dao learning in the activity with other methods before and after the activity, mending the top-down versus bottom-up divisions.

The Daoists and Dewey use the environment to regulate the learning between student and lesson activity, but the different roles for the teachers create differences in the lesson steps. In the Daoist approach, the teacher focuses on the absences in the set-up, non-action in the activity, and exchange in the closing step. Dewey's teacher focuses on choosing content for growth in the set-up, guidance in the activity, and evaluation in the closing.

The environments that regulate the learning are different. The Daoist environment is natural, while Dewey's is structured by purpose. The differences suggest that there will be more diversity in the outcomes in the dao lesson than in Dewey's. They also suggest that when teaching dao lessons, the teacher will hold even higher values for self-directed learning and one's ability to solve problems on one's own compared to Dewey's teacher.

Teachers need time to practice teaching dao lessons and to shift some of the views they hold about teaching and learning. Students also need time to adjust to the openness in the process. Some might initially interpret it for doing what one wants, and some might want to be told what to learn. Realizing the dao process takes time, but once achieved, it will display its many benefits.

The basic dao lesson defines the main structures in each step. These are used to guide the designs for the variations in the following chapters.

Chapter Summary

The main characteristics of the Daoist approach to lesson design are as follows:

- The characteristics of dao learning and teaching practices are used to design a 3-step lesson plan.
- The objective in the basic lesson is for students to develop new ideas on their own.
- In the set-up step, the teacher makes sure that the students have knowledge of all of the participants in the planned lesson. (The students' past knowledge can be taught using any method.)
- The teacher plans a lesson activity ensuring the absences.
- In the lesson activity, the interaction is between students and the lesson environment. The teacher practices non-action.
- In the closing step, students continue their learning by exploring their new ideas in different contexts. (The teaching methods are open.)
- It is rare to give homework in a dao lesson.
- Dao lessons can easily be applied to regular lessons.
- The different teaching practices in the Daoist and Dewey's approaches affect the character of the steps and outcomes.

Sidelight: Nature Learning

Way-making (*dao*) gives things their life,
And their particular efficacy (*de*) is what nurtures them.
Events shape them,
And having a function consummates them.
It is for this reason that all things (*wanwu*) honor way-making
And esteem efficacy.
As for the honor directed at way-making
And the esteem directed at efficacy,
It is really something that just happens spontaneously (*ziran*)
Without anyone having ennobled them.

Daodejing, chapter 51[45]

CHAPTER 6

Lesson Variations: Open Outcomes

Way-making gives things life
Yet does not manage them.
It assists them
Yet makes no claim upon them.
It rears them
Yet does not lord it over them.
It is this that is called profound efficacy.

Daodejing, chapter 51[46]

Open Variations

'Yet makes no claim upon them,' describes the open outcomes of the lesson variations presented in this chapter. An open outcome is not predetermined, not evaluated, and is unique to each student.

These variations are used when the teacher wants to use dao learning with an outcome open to each student's creation.

The criteria in the variations are the same as in the basic lesson. The lessons follow the characteristics of dao learning and absence practices, protecting the unworked wood. However, while ensuring these conditions, the teacher can adjust the steps for different lesson objectives. In the basic dao lesson, the teacher wants students to learn new material on their own, but in the open variations, the teacher wants the outcomes to be fully open to the students' creations.

This chapter gives three variations with open outcomes. It describes the steps in each variation and gives example lessons.

Variations with Open Outcomes

The open outcome variation lessons are used when the teacher wants students to use what they have learned in their own way, to explore relationships among the participants of a unit of study, or to practice the dao learning process.

The three variations are:

Variation 1: Taking turns
Variation 2: Structuring a unit
Variation 3: Practicing the arts

Variation 1: Taking Turns

The variation is called 'taking turns' as the teacher and students take turns working with the material in a unit of study.

This variation is used when the teacher wants students to use the material that they have learned to create personal outcomes.

Step 1: Set-up

In both the 'taking turns' and basic lesson set-up, the teacher reviews the students' knowledge to determine if it includes all of the participants in the planned learning situation. However, in this variation, the students' past knowledge is not to be used to develop new ideas as in the basic lesson, but to be used by students in their own way. When the teacher determines that the students have access to all of the participants, the teacher plans the activity with the absences.

Step 2: Lesson Activity

The teacher might begin the lesson with a review and then introduce the activity. From that point on, students work on their own and the teacher practices non-action.

Step 3: Closing

The outcomes are the students' creations.

The closing step follows the structure of the basic lesson with students continuing their learning by sharing their individual creations with other students and the teacher. The teacher is an active participant in this step, can lead discussions, and can also give a presentation of related material.

Example Lesson

Lesson: Textile construction for high school students

Students make a wall hanging.

Situation

Students have learned:

Plain weave
Twill weave
Satin weave
Knits
Bonding

The various types of textile construction have been taught using any teaching method. The methods might include demonstrations of how yarns are combined, pictures of fabrics, viewing fabrics under a microscope, reading assignments, and making samples with paper strips. The unit of study is completed.

Lesson

Step 1: Set-up

The teacher identifies the participants in the planned lesson.
The teacher reviews what the students have learned about textile construction.
The teacher determines that the unit of study is completed, and the students have knowledge of all of the lesson participants.
The teacher plans an activity with the absences.
The activity is for students to make a wall hanging using any material and construction method. Students are given a week to collect their material.

Step 2: Lesson Activity

The teacher opens with a review of the activity objective.
The students work on their own.
The teacher practices non-action.

Step 3: Closing

The students display their wall hangings and view other students' work. The hangings include:

Yarns with branches
Yarns and feathers
Combinations of weaves, colours, and yarn sizes
Strips of fabrics in different weaves
Figures in the weaves
Paper and plastic, yarns and beads

The teacher leads a discussion and shows pictures of several textile displays in the city.

Variation 2: Structuring a Unit

This variation is called 'structuring a unit' as the dao lesson is used to structure a unit of study. It is considered at the beginning of a unit of study when the teacher wants students to explore relationships among the participants of the unit. How each student views the relationships is open.

Step 1: Set-up

The basic and 'taking turns' lessons require students to have the knowledge of the participants in the activity, but this variation is planned at the beginning of a unit of study. The teacher can still provide the knowledge for each of the participants of the unit, but ensures the absences in the relationships among the parts.

This variation can be done in one lesson, or can be used to structure learning over a period of time.

Step 2: Lesson Activity

The teacher might begin the lesson with a review and then introduce a new part of the unit of study using any teaching method. Students explore how each part relates to other parts on their own.

Step 3: Closing

The outcomes are the students' views of how the parts of the unit are related. The closing step follows the structure of the basic lesson with students continuing their learning by sharing their individual ideas with other students and the teacher. The teacher is an active participant in this step, can lead discussions, and can also give a presentation related to the study.

Example Lesson

Lesson: Classroom tasks for any grade level

Students develop an understanding of classroom tasks.

The teacher wants the students to do the classroom tasks, but when using the 'structuring a unit' lesson, the objective is for students to develop an understanding of how each task works with other tasks to contribute to the functioning of the unit.

Situation

Students have learned:

Students have some background experience in classroom tasks, but their knowledge varies.

Lesson

Step 1: Set-up

The teacher reviews the tasks: attendance taker, trash monitor, board eraser, etc. (tasks adjusted for grade level).

The teacher reviews what the students have learned about classroom tasks.

The teacher determines that the students have some knowledge, but it varies.

The teacher plans the activity ensuring the absences. All tasks must be in their state of genuineness and considered equal participants in the unit of study.

Therefore, students cannot choose the tasks that interest them. The teacher cannot choose students for the tasks, assign tasks as rewards or punishments, or give them according to specific student qualifications.

The teacher describes each task on a card. Students will be given a task and will rotate their tasks every two weeks so that each student will learn all of the tasks. The lesson will start at the beginning of the school year and continue throughout the year.

Step 2: Lesson Activity

The teacher introduces the activity.

The students receive their tasks and rotate them every two weeks.

The teacher does not interfere in the task routine.

Step 3: Closing

The teacher will periodically lead discussions so that students can share their ideas. The teacher also gives examples of relationships in various school activities.

Variation 3: Practicing the Arts

The third open variation uses the arts to practice the dao process. The arts are considered creative fields, and as such, are excellent ways for students to develop a disposition for the dao process.

When using the arts to practice the dao process extra care must be taken, as simply doing an art activity does not necessarily express the dao process. The teacher must ensure the absences in the activity and leave the outcome open.

Step 1: Set-up

The 'practicing the arts' variation begins with the teacher determining if students have the knowledge of all the participants in the planned learning situation. The students' past knowledge is to be used by students in their own way. When this is determined, the teacher plans an art activity with the absences.

Step 2: Lesson Activity

The teacher might begin the lesson with a review and then introduce the activity. As in all dao lessons, students work on their own and the teacher practices non-action.

Step 3: Closing

The outcomes are the students' development of a natural relationship with their environment.

The closing step follows the structure of the basic lesson. Students share their individual creations with other students and the teacher. The teacher is an active participant in this step, can lead discussions, and might also give a presentation of related material.

Example Lesson

Lesson: Painting class for any grade level

Students paint a picture.

Situation

Students have learned:

Drawing
Brush techniques
Mixing colours

Basic painting skills have been taught using any teaching method. The methods might include demonstrations, studies of paintings, required reading, videos, and practice.

Lesson

Step 1: Set-up

The teacher identifies the participants in the planned lesson.
The teacher reviews what the students have learned in their painting classes.
The teacher determines that the students have the painting skills for the activity.
The teacher plans an activity with the absences.
The activity is for students to make a painting of a bowl of fruit.
The teacher prepares the materials.

Step 2: Lesson Activity

The teacher opens with a review and outlines the activity.
The students work on their paintings.
The teacher practices non-action.

Step 3: Closing

The students display their finished paintings and view other students' work.
The teacher leads a discussion and shows pictures of paintings of fruit.

Discussion

The steps in the basic dao lesson plan are changed to give three variations with open outcomes—'taking turns,' 'structuring a unit,' and 'practicing the arts.' The learning objective in the variations is for students to create their own outcomes.

While the lesson outcomes are open to students' creations, the lesson objectives differ. The teacher might want to encourage students to use what they have learned in their own way, gain an understanding of relationships among the participants in a unit of study, or use the arts to practice the dao process. The teacher can plan the lesson at the end of a unit of study or at the beginning. The lesson can be for one activity or it can be ongoing.

The example lessons in the chapter show how easy it is for teachers to apply the dao lessons to current lessons with a few adjustments.

The open outcomes also highlight one of the main differences with Dewey's lesson—the lesson objectives. This difference is exemplified in a comparison of Dewey's portrayal of an artist at work, which resembles the dao process, and his description of an art lesson. In the lesson, the teacher evaluates the student's drawing, and the student then remakes it according to the teacher's input.[47]

In all of the variations, the teacher practices non-action. This can be a challenging practice to cultivate, however, as in the basic lesson, it is important to remember that the non-action is used to fulfill a particular lesson objective, and other teaching methods can be used before and after the activity.

The next chapter gives two variations for outcomes that are defined by input from both the teacher and student.

Chapter Summary

The main characteristics of open variation lessons are as follows:

- Changes can be made in the three steps of the basic dao lesson providing the conditions for dao learning are ensured.
- The three open variations presented in this chapter are 'taking turns,' 'structuring a unit,' and 'practicing the arts.'
- The learning objective in these variations is an outcome open to each student's creation.
- The lesson can be at the end of a unit of study or at the beginning, for one activity or ongoing.
- The teacher practices non-action in the activity.
- The closing step follows the basic lesson structure to continue learning.
- The arts can be used to practice the dao process.
- The open outcomes in the lessons highlight the difference in objectives in the Daoist and Dewey's lessons.

Sidelight: The Sage in the Child

Confucius asked Lao Tzu, "since you're sitting here at peace in the sunshine within your own gates this day, may I ask you about getting to the Tao?"

"The most learned may not know this, the logician may not find its sweet solution. And so the sage breaks with learning and logic. What can be poured into without ever overflowing? What can be drawn from without ever emptying? That is what the sage holds to. Deep, deep is the source, so like the sea. And lofty like mountains. When its string is run out, it is born to begin again. It moves all the ten thousand things along, never failing. That Way of the Gentleman of yours is a long way from this. What the ten thousand things keep coming to for help—and never leave wanting—that is what the Tao is."

Zhuangzi, chapter 22[48]

CHAPTER 7

Lesson Variations: Mixed Outcomes

Know the clean
Yet safeguard the soiled
And be a valley to the world.
As a valley to the world
Your real potency will be ample,
And with ample potency,
You return to the state of unworked wood.

Daodejing, chapter 28[49]

Mixed Variations

'Your real potency will be ample,' even when being inclusive of the world. In the mixed variations, being inclusive can still leave students with the potency of unworked wood.

The variations combine the polarities of top-down and bottom-up teaching practices in a dao learning activity. The teacher defines specific material for the outcome, and uses dao learning to characterize the lesson. The outcomes are the students' creations of the material.

Like the basic lesson, the teacher wants students to learn new material, but instead of having them develop the material on their own, the teacher gives the material to the students. The teacher can still design a lesson with the absences to ensure dao learning.

This chapter gives two variations with mixed outcomes. It describes the steps in each variation and gives example lessons.

Variations with Mixed Outcomes

The mixed variation lessons are used when the teacher wants a learning activity to include one part defined by the teacher and the other part defined by the students, or an activity in which the material is fully defined by the teacher but the interactions with this material are defined by the students.

The two variations are:

Variation 4: Minimum specs
Variation 5: Creative repetition

Variation 4: Minimum Specs

This variation lesson is called 'minimum specs' because the teacher specifies a minimum amount of material to be learned in an activity and leaves students to decide on the remaining part. This variation is considered when the teacher wants students to learn fixed material, but also wants students to explore it on their own terms. The outcome is a mixture of the two.

Step 1: Set-up

In the 'minimum specs,' the teacher specifies what is to be learned in the activity. The part of the activity that is specified must be a minimum amount in order to let the students decide on the other parts of the activity. The teacher plans an activity that includes these two elements.

Step 2: Lesson Activity

The teacher might begin the lesson with a review and then introduce the activity. The activity will include the fixed material to be learned. From that point on, students work on their own and the teacher practices non-action.

Step 3: Closing

The outcomes are the students' creations of the fixed material.

The closing step follows the structure of the basic lesson with students continuing their learning by sharing their outcomes with other students and the teacher. The teacher is an active participant in this step, can lead a discussion, and can also give a presentation of related material.

Example Lesson

Lesson: Flower arranging for upper grade levels

Students learn a flower arrangement form.

Situation

Students have learned:

Basic flower arranging skills, such as how to cut branches and flowers
Basic arrangement forms

The basic skills have been taught using any teaching method. The methods might include demonstrations, reading assignments, and practice.
Students have a text describing the flower arrangement forms.

Lesson

Step 1: Set-up

The teacher reviews the arrangement form to be learned.
The teacher reviews what the students have learned.
The teacher determines that they have the skills needed to make the new arrangement.
The teacher plans an activity with the absences.
The new arrangement form is the 'minimum specs.' The students will reference the text for a description of the form (students know how to read). The rest of the activity is decided by the students. The students will choose their vase, branches, and flowers.
The teacher prepares an assortment of flowers and branches, and checks the supply of vases.

Step 2: Lesson Activity

The teacher opens with a review and gives the arrangement form to be learned.
Students choose their materials.
The students work on their own following the instructions in the text.
The teacher practices non-action.

Step 3: Closing

The teacher checks the form in each student's arrangement. This can include discussions.
The students view other students' arrangements. There is variation in the arrangements despite the form being the same.
The teacher gives a demonstration. This gives students a view of their goals in flower arranging.

Variation 5: Creative Repetition

Repetition is not a technique that is considered creative from a progressive perspective, but it has been studied as a method of learning with dao. The 'creative repetition' variation takes the process of repetition from simple rote to a creative process.

It is used when the teacher has specific material to be learned that requires practice, and wants the practice activity to be defined by dao learning. Students' outcomes are a mixture of the material and the relationships that they develop with the material.

Each time the student repeats the material, the relationship with the material is modified. The modification is most constructive if done in different contexts.

Ding practicing his butchering skills for many years is an example of creative repetition, as is Eugen Herrigel's description of the art of archery.

Step 1: Set-up

In the 'creative repetition' variation, the teacher wants students to repeat what has been taught. The teacher plans an activity ensuring the absences.

Step 2: Lesson Activity

The teacher might begin the lesson with a review and then introduce the activity. From that point on, students work on their own and the teacher practices non-action.

Step 3: Closing

The outcomes are the students' creations of the specified material.

The closing step continues the learning with students sharing their outcomes with other students and the teacher. The teacher is an active participant in this step, can lead discussions, and can also give a presentation of the material or related material.

In this variation, individual practice outside of the lesson time is usually part of the learning process.

Example Lesson

Lesson: Tango dance for any grade level

Students practice the tango.

Situation

Students have learned:

The Argentine tango 8-step basic

The 8-step basic of the Argentine tango has been taught using any teaching method. The methods might include demonstrations, assigned reading, practice, and videos.

Lesson

Step 1: Set-up

The teacher reviews the dance steps in the planned lesson.

The teacher reviews what the students have learned.

The teacher determines that the students have learned the steps of the basic dance.

The teacher plans an activity with the absences.

Students will perform the dance to music.

The teacher selects the music and will change it several times in the lesson so that the students can practice the dance in different contexts.

Step 2: Lesson Activity

The teacher reviews the steps and outlines the activity.

The students practice the dance.

The teacher practices non-action except to change the music.

Step 3: Closing

Each pair performs their dance for other students. The teacher leads discussions.

The teacher gives a demonstration of the dance.

The teacher encourages students to practice the steps outside of lesson time.

Discussion

The mixed outcome variations are different from the basic and open lessons as the teacher defines either part or the whole of the material in the outcomes. The objective in the variations is for the students' outcomes to be their creations of the material. The chapter gives two variations with mixed outcomes—'minimum specs' and 'creative repetition.'

The teacher defines part or all of the material to be learned in the activity. When in part, students contribute the remaining part, and when all of the material is given, they learn by repetition on their own terms. Although these variations begin as top-down instruction with the teacher specifying what is to be learned, conditions can still be set up to include each student's unique contribution and outcome.

The teacher can apply the mixed variations to regular lessons as shown in the example lessons with adjustments to ensure the conditions for dao learning. Combining dao learning with top-down instruction follows the Daoist idea that opposites actually work together. The mixed variations show how dao learning can dovetail with other methods not only in the before and after of the activity, but in the activity itself.

The mixed lessons are different from Dewey's experience as they include top-down instruction to define the outcomes. Although there is no top-down instruction in Dewey's lesson, there is a desired outcome. And, although there is top-down instruction in the two variations, they are open to students' creations.

The mixed variations are guides showing different ways to design dao lessons for teaching specific material.

Chapter Summary

The main characteristics of mixed variation lessons are as follows:

- The two mixed variations presented in this chapter are 'minimum specs' and 'creative repetition.'
- The learning objective is for students to learn specific material with their creative input.
- The teacher begins by defining a part or the whole of the material to be learned in the activity.
- Students contribute by defining a part of the activity or by learning through repetition when the teacher specifies the whole.
- In the lesson activity, students work on their own and the teacher practices non-action.
- The closing step follows the basic lesson structure to continue learning.
- The 'creative repetition' variation encourages practice outside of lesson time.
- The mixed variations reveal the possibility for more diverse outcomes than in Dewey's lessons despite the use of top-down instruction.

Sidelight: Knowing Enough

When way-making (*dao*) prevails in the world,
The finest racing steeds are used to provide manure for the fields;
But when way-making does not prevail in the world,
Warhorses are bred just outside the city walls. . . .

Thus, knowing when enough is enough
Is really satisfying.

Daodejing, chapter 46[50]

CHAPTER 8

Teaching Dao Lessons in Context

What has been well-planted cannot be uprooted;
What is embraced tightly will not escape one's grasp;
And with one's children and grandchildren performing the
    customary rites
The autumnal sacrifice will never be interrupted.
Cultivate it in your person,
And the character you develop will be genuine; . . .

How do I know that the world is really so?
From this.

Daodejing, chapter 54[51]

Fulfilling the Promise of Nature

'What has been well-planted cannot be uprooted,' when one looks to nature as the most specialized and powerful path to guide our becoming process. We now understand that the process is not confined to particular aspects of our world, but rather it governs and defines all matter including humans and their minds.

The Dao of Teaching presents a Daoist view of teaching and learning that offers a way to bring nature to lessons. It defines the criteria for dao learning and provides practical lesson examples to assist teachers in applying them.

The basic lesson and the five variations in the chapters are guides for teachers to consider the dao lessons in different circumstances. The examples show that changing a regular lesson to a dao lesson needs only a few alterations, but these few can make a difference in the character of the learning. Teachers can review the exercises in chapter 2 and see what shifts in values and perspectives are needed to design a dao lesson. And, with an understanding of dao learning in lessons, they can choose to use one or all of the examples, use the dao lessons occasionally or frequently, or they can design their own dao lessons.

Teaching dao lessons does not discount the power of gardens, forests, and various contemplative techniques that serve the same purpose. It is a way of using the lesson as Eng's garden, 'to open your mind, to lead you to the heart of a contemplative state,' to be 'awakened to something higher, something timeless.' The teaching also does not dismiss the contributions and beauty of the intellection or rites of our ancestors, and their passing to the next generation as the drawstring of dao. It does, however, question the divisiveness and efficacy of the top-down and bottom-up polarities that Zhuangzi describes as the ongoing flip-flop of 'this and that.'[52]

If we were to look for a central idea that defines the Daoist approach in education, we might say that it is the focus on protecting the innate in the relationship between humans and their environment. It is the acknowledgement of and deference for the innate in all, as well as its past and its future of ten thousand things.

The Daoists express this focus in the absences. Teachers understanding and using the absences to promote the natural relationship also express this focus. It is bringing the promise of nature to children to see, understand, and live in their world.

The message of nature comes to us in increasingly troubled and uncertain times, in a world in which humans have become separated from nature, in a world in which nature's actions are thrown into convulsions. But despite this separation, we can find the way of nature in the verses preserved in the *Daodejing*. The text, Ames and Hall tell us, was written for the very purpose of restoring society in times of trouble, in times of war and death, in times when humans live separate from nature.[53]

Teaching lessons with dao is experimenting, repeating, and sharing in the creation of the myriad of possibilities to bring nature to the children. The children need to develop all ways to navigate in the future of unknowns, and as educators and tenants of the earth, this is our job.

Sidelight: Reassuring the Latest Child

I wish to speak a word for Nature, for absolute freedom and wildness, as contrasted with a freedom and culture merely civil—to regard man as an inhabitant, or a part and parcel of Nature, rather than a member of society.

I took a walk on Spaulding's Farm the other afternoon. . . . They seemed to recline on the sunbeams. They have sons and daughters. They are quite well. . . . Nothing can equal the serenity of their lives. Their coat-of-arms is simply a lichen. I saw it painted on the pines and oaks. Their attics were in the tops of the trees.

It was such a light as we could not have imagined a moment before, and the air also was so warm and serene that nothing was wanting to make a paradise of that meadow. When we reflected that this was not a solitary phenomenon, never to happen again, but that it would happen forever and ever, an infinite number of evenings, and cheer and reassure the latest child that walked there, it was more glorious still.

'Walking'[54]

Endnotes

1. Ames & Hall (2003):156–157.
2. de Bary (2008):15.
3. Ames & Hall (2003):77–79.
4. Dewey (1925/2008):47.
5. Grange (2004):89. See also Ames & Hall (2003), Kobayashi (1962), Maki (2016), and Zigler (2007).
6. The lesson designs are based on the following:
   Chapters 2 and 5:
   The mathematics lesson is from an example by T. Takahashi, Tokyo Gakugei University. See also Maki (2019) and Stigler & Hiebert (1999).
   Chapter 6:
   Variation 1 'taking turns' is from the author's teaching experiences. Variation 2 'structuring a unit' is from Fruin (1997), Maki (2001), and Morgan (1977). Variation 3 'practicing the arts' is from Chang (1963/2011) and Xiaoyuan & Lin (2012).
   Chapter 7:
   Variation 4 'minimum specs' is from the author's art classes and conference paper (2016), Fruin (1997), and Morgan (1977). The term is taken from Morgan. Variation 5 'creative repetition' is from examples in Herrigel (1953/1989) and Zigler (2007).
7. Taken from Hamill & Seaton (1999):22–26.
8. Hamill & Seaton (1999):21.
9. Ames & Hall (2003):90.
10. This exercise is based on the U.S. Department of Education Schools and Staffing Survey (SASS) Teacher Questionnaire, 1990-91, #38. The first seven goals on the list are from the questionnaire and the last two were added to cover goals that might correspond with learner-directed learning and the current goal of sustainability.

11. Thoreau (1854/2017):31.
12. Ames & Hall (2003):115.
13. Taken from Ames & Hall (2003):57–59.
14. Chen (1989):52.
15. Ames & Hall (2003):77–79.
16. Taken from Hamill & Seaton (1999):19–20.
17. Capra (1987):11 and 269.
18. Ames & Hall (2003):18–19.
19. Ames & Hall (2003):78.
20. Ames & Hall (2003):91.
21. See also attunement in Maki (2016):160.
22. Ames & Hall (2003):80 and 96.
23. Ames & Hall (2003):80.
24. Ni (1995):1, 5, and 8.
25. Ames & Hall (2003):166.
26. Ames & Hall (2003):80.
27. Ames & Hall (2003):80. See also *wuwei* in Slingerland (2014).
28. Ames & Hall (2003):82.
29. Watson (1968/2013):197.
30. Ames & Hall (2003):80.
31. Taken from Ames & Hall (2003):227; de Bary (2008):68.
32. Ames & Hall (2003):136.
33. Taken from Watson (1968/2013):190–193.
34. Ames & Hall (2003):149.
35. Ames & Hall (2003):122.
36. Dewey (1925/2008):228.
37. Ames & Hall (2003):81.
38. Ames & Hall (2003):159.
39. Eng (2012):277.
40. Dewey (1938/1963):83.
41. Dewey (1900/1990):129.
42. Dewey (1902/1990):195.
43. Ames & Hall (2003):183.
44. Ames & Hall (2003):187–188.
45. Ames & Hall (2003):156.

46. Ames & Hall (2003):157.
47. Dewey (1900/1990):40–43.
48. Hamill & Seaton (1999):124–125.
49. Ames & Hall (2003):120.
50. Ames & Hall (2003):149.
51. Ames & Hall (2003):160–161.
52. Hamill & Seaton (1999):11, in chapter 'All Things Being Equal.'
53. Ames & Hall (2003):1–2.
54. Thoreau (1862).

Bibliography of Works Cited

Ames, R. T., & Hall, D. L. (2003). *Daodejing: Making this life significant*. Ballantine Books.

Capra, F. (1987). *The Tao of physics*. London: Flamingo.

Chang, C. (2011). *Creativity and Taoism: A study of Chinese philosophy, art, and poetry*. Singing Dragon. (Original work published in 1963).

Chen, E. M. (1989). *Tao Te Ching*. Paragon House.

de Bary, W. T. (Ed.). (2008). *Sources of East Asian tradition* (Vol. 1). Columbia University Press.

Dewey, J. (1934). *Art as experience*. Minton, Balch.

————. (1963). *Experience and education*. Collier Books. (Original work published in 1938).

————. (1990). *The school and society and The child and the curriculum*. The University of Chicago Press. (Original work published in 1900 and 1902).

————. (2008). *Experience and nature*. In J. A. Boydston (Ed.), *John Dewey: The later works* (Vol. 1). Southern Illinois University Press. (Original work published in 1925).

Eng, T. T. (2012). *The garden of evening mists*. Weinstein Books.

Fruin, W. M. (1997). *Knowledge works: Managing intellectual capital at Toshiba*. Oxford University Press.

Grange, J. (2004). *John Dewey, Confucius, and global philosophy*. State University of New York Press.

Hamill S., & Seaton J. P. (Trans.). (1999). *The essential Chuang Tzu*. Shambhala.

Herrigel, E. (1989). *Zen in the art of archery* (D. T. Suzuki, Introduction; R. F. C. Hull, Trans.). Vintage Books. (Original work published in 1953).

Kobayashi, V. (1962). The quest for experience: Zen, Dewey, and education. *Comparative Education Review*, 5(3), 217–222.

Maki W. J. (2001). *Schools as learning organizations: How Japanese teachers learn to perform non-instructional tasks* [Doctoral dissertation, University of British Columbia].

————. (2016). Dewey's link with Daoism: Ideals of nature, cultivation practices, and applications in lessons. *Educational Philosophy and Theory,* 48(2), 150–164.

————. (2016, March 6–10). *Daoism and education: Exploring the influence of Daoism on teachers' practices in ikebana classes in Japan* [Paper presentation]. Comparative and International Education Society (CIES) Conference 2016, Vancouver, BC, Canada.

————. (2019, April 14–18). *Daoism in education: Exploring nature as a metaphor for teaching and learning* [Round table presentation]. Comparative and International Education Society (CIES) Conference 2019, San Francisco, CA, United States.

Morgan, G. (1977). *Images of organization* (2nd ed.). Sage Publications.

Ni, M. (Trans.). (1995). *The Yellow Emperor's classic of medicine*: *A new translation of the Neijing Suwen with commentary*. Shambhala.

Rousseau, J. J. (1974). *Émile* (P. D. Jimack, Introduction; B. Foxley, Trans.). Charles E. Tuttle. (Original title published in 1911).

Slingerland, E. (2014). *Trying not to try*: *The art and science of spontaneity*. Crown.

Stigler, J. W., & Hiebert J. (1999). *The teaching gap: Best ideas from the world's teachers for improving education in the classroom*. The Free Press.

Thoreau, H. D. (1862, June). Walking. *The Atlantic Monthly*, 9(56), 657–674. Retrieved from https://www.theatlantic.com/magazine/archive/1862/06/walkin g/304674/

————. (2017). *Walden* (B. McKibben, Introduction). Beacon Press. (Original work published in 1854).

U.S. Department of Education, National Center for Education Statistics (1993). *Schools and staffing in the United States: A statistical profile, 1990–91.*

Watson, B. (Trans.). (2013). *The complete works of Zhuangzi.* Columbia University Press. (Original work published in 1968 as *The complete works of Chuang Tzu*).

Xiaoyuan, S., & Lin, J. (2012). Daoism and Chinese landscape painting: Implications for education for human-nature harmony. In R. L. Oxford & J. Lin (Eds.), *Transformative eco-education for human and planetary survival* (335–347). Information Age Publishing.

Zigler, R. L. (2007). The Tao of Dewey. *Encounter*, 20(1), 37–42.

Index

absence approach, 56
Ames, R. T., & Hall, D. L.
  becoming process, 9, 30
  dao-ing, way-making, 30
  educational perspective, 8
  energy of transformation, 34
  human imagination, 33
  mirroring activity, 54
  soup imagery, 32
  verse reference, ix
application of absences, 51–53
attunement, 34
authenticity, 3, 45
basic dao lesson, 63–66
benefits, dao learning, 3, 70
butcher Cook Ding
  reference to, 31, 32, 34, 38, 92
  story, 31
Capra, F.
  quantum mechanics, 10, 28,
    31, 39
China, 6
Confucius, 6, 12, 86
creative repetition variation, 92
dao learning
  and Dewey's artist, 33
  as dao process. *See* dao
    process
  benefits, 3
  description, 33–35
  dovetails, 37
  education goal, 101
  energy of transformation, 34
  genuineness in, 34
  in lessons, 36
  interaction part, 34

  outcome part, 35
  past part, 34
dao process
  and Cook Ding, 31
  becoming process, 30
  creation in nature, 29
  description, 31–32
  humans take part, 38
  non-being to being, 31, 32
  practicing the arts, 81
  quantum mechanics, 31
  three parts, 32
  unity of opposites, 36
dao, written character, 29
Daodejing
  and Laozi, 6
  application procedures, 51
  dao defined, 29
  educational interpretation, 8
  in the West, 6
  instructions to the sages, 42
  restorative, 101
  teaching practices defined, 44
  verse reference, ix
Daoism, philosophy
  based on nature, 6
  educational treatise, 2
  humans and environment, 8
  in the West, 6
  main texts, 6
  origins, 6
  resource for nature, 8
  resource in education, 8
Dewey, J.
  and Lao-tzu, 9
  artist, 33, 34, 38, 50, 84

Acknowledgments

The processual of our experiences that bring us to our present understanding includes so many aspects, not the least of which is the work of many scholars. My interpretations in this project are grounded in such contributions, and especially the work of my doctoral advisor Mark Fruin, the interpretation of the *Daodejing* by Roger T. Ames and David L. Hall (and with verses reprinted with the kind permission of Roger Ames), the helpful comments of colleagues, and the guidance and work of Victor Kobayashi. Also, my friends and family cannot be forgotten for their support on my journey of searching.

Over time the verses of the *Daodejing* have become images of beauty, joy, and hope that have inspired an interpretation of the philosophy that offers possibilities to bring nature to children's learning. Ideas for teaching and learning based on the Daoist view of nature have been tested in my classes and presented on various international education platforms. This has cumulated in developing a plan for presenting an introduction to Daoism as an educational treatise, the theory of dao learning and teaching, and example lesson plans.

About the Author

Wilma J. Maki's early research on East Asian history and education led to her interest in Daoism as a resource in education. Her studies and experiences teaching have inspired an interpretation of the philosophy that offers possibilities to bring nature to children's learning.

www.ingramcontent.com/pod-product-compliance
Lightning Source LLC
Chambersburg PA
CBHW060805110426
42739CB00032BA/3095